VIRGINIA WOOLF
and Monk's House

East Sussex

National Trust

'An unpretending house'

On 26 June 1919 Virginia Woolf and her husband, Leonard, spotted a notice in an auctioneer's in Lewes: 'Lot 1. Monks House, Rodmell. An old fashioned house standing in three quarters of an acre of land to be sold with possession'. Although they had just bought a house in Lewes, having been forced to give up nearby Asheham House, which Virginia had been renting since 1911, they decided to take a look. Virginia's first impressions were not encouraging:

> "These rooms are small, I said to myself; you must discount the value of that old chimney piece & the niches for holy water. Monks are nothing out of the way. The kitchen is distinctly bad. There's an oil stove, & no grate. Nor is there hot water, nor a bath, & as for the E.C. [earth closet] I was never shown it. These prudent objections kept excitement at bay; yet even they were forced to yield place to a profound pleasure at the size & shape & fertility & wildness of the garden".

They decided to bid, and at a tense auction on 1 July acquired Monk's House for £700.

'That will be our address for ever and ever', Virginia declared, and so it proved. Monk's House became a welcome country retreat from London – for weekends, for Easter and Christmas, and for long stretches in the summer. In 1919 she was 37, her first novel, *The Voyage Out*, had been published four years earlier, and she was anxiously correcting the proofs of her second, *Night and Day*. Over the next two decades, the details of the Sussex landscape

Monk's House from the road: 'but the point of it is the garden'

and of village life in Rodmell fed into her work, and are expressed perhaps most fully in her last novel, *Between the Acts* (1941).

Virginia said, 'There is little ceremony or precision at Monks House. It is an unpretending house, long & low, a house of many doors', and even by the austere standards of Bloomsbury, life here was uncomfortable. The kitchen flooded on the first night. When E.M. Forster came to stay, he was so cold that he burnt his trousers trying to get warm beside the 'Cozy Stove' in his bedroom. Gradually, however, with the financial success of Virginia's novels, the Woolfs were able to make improvements to the house. The Kitchen was rebuilt, and a bath and hot water were installed; *Mrs Dalloway and The Common Reader* paid for two new water-closets in 1925 (both dedicated to Virginia's friend, Vita Sackville-West); and in 1929 they added a two-storey extension. In 1931 Virginia could write that 'the house was luxurious to the point of [having] electric fires in the bedrooms'.

'I could fancy a very pleasant walk in the orchard under the apple trees, with the grey extinguisher of the church steeple pointing my boundary' (diary, 3 July 1919)

Asheham House, about 1924; by Fred Porter (Bedroom): 'Ah but how happy we've been at Asheham! It was a most melodious time. Everything went so freely' (diary, 5 May 1919)

Life at Monk's House

When the Woolfs had no visitors, Virginia's life fell into a regular routine. Over a leisurely breakfast in bed, brought up on a tray by Leonard, she read her post. Then she took a bath; in the kitchen directly below, their cook Louie Everest could hear Virginia talking to herself. As Leonard explained, 'She always said the sentences out loud that she had written during the night. She needed to know if they sounded right and the bath was a good resonant place for trying them out'. Then she would write or correct for three hours in her writing-lodge in the garden, if the weather was fine.

After a simple lunch, perhaps of a rissole and a custard, she would read for a couple of hours and smoke. She rolled her own cigarettes, preferring a mild blend known as 'My Mixture'. Then she would open the garden gate and take a walk out towards the South Downs, 'where all nature is to be had in five minutes', often getting as far as Asheham on the other side of the Ouse Valley. She loved this landscape, both understanding and deploring the reasons why it was gradually being invaded by the modern world, of which she was herself one symptom: their garage had once been the village forge. Walking also helped her to get the right rhythm into her sentences.

She had tea at four, and then wrote her copious letters and diary: 'We sit over the fire, waiting for the post – the cream of the day, I think'. After supper, they would listen to music on the gramophone in the Sitting Room. In his diary, Leonard meticulously noted every record they played.

Leonard at his writing desk at Monk's House; painted by Vanessa Bell in 1940 (National Portrait Gallery)

Monk's House gave Virginia the space and the peace to think and write, and soon became an essential part of her life, 'after the fashion of a mongrel who wins your heart'.

And when there were visitors, there was always conversation, as John Lehmann recalled:

What was young X writing? Was it true that So-and-So had broken his best friend's marriage? What did we think of the latest magazine? The latest production of *The Duchess of Malfi* or *Twelfth Night*? What on earth was she to answer to the old bore Z, who kept on writing her pompous fan-letters from America? She delighted in witty gossip, and would discuss the comic and tragic events of the day as keenly as the deepest problems of literature. There can never have been anyone on whom the mantle of acknowledged literary greatness lay less heavily.

'We tend our fire, cook coffee, read, I find, luxuriously, peacefully, at length' (diary, 7 January 1920). Virginia is sitting in the upstairs sitting-room (not shown to visitors)

Vanessa Bell's 1939 oil sketch of the Woolfs' cocker spaniel, Sally, which also appears in her portrait of Leonard. Sally was particularly fond of Leonard

Furnishing Monk's House

The fireplace tiles in the Bedroom were painted by Vanessa for her sister in 1930

With the house, the Woolfs bought some furniture, cutlery, a mass of garden tools, and three naive portraits of the Glazebrooks, a family of millers who had lived at Monk's House in the 19th century and left the millstones now incorporated into the garden paths.

Virginia painted the walls herself in shades of blue, yellow, pomegranate and a violent green that drew sarcastic comments from her relatives. In her choice of new furnishings, she relied heavily on her sister, the painter Vanessa Bell, who from 1916 transformed Charleston farmhouse five miles away into the most complete expression of Bloomsbury visual taste, with her fellow-painter, Duncan Grant. The Woolfs filled their house with paintings, textiles and pottery created by Duncan and Vanessa, and furniture in the style of the Omega Workshops, which had been run by Vanessa's friend, the art critic and painter Roger Fry, from 1913 to 1919. They also bought furniture and painted earthenware on summer holidays in the South of France. Much of the statuary in the garden came from a general store in Barcombe.

However, Monk's House was always the home of writers rather than art collectors. The damage that damp Asheham was causing their books had almost reconciled Virginia to leaving it. Books came first, and after their London home was bombed in 1940, Monk's House was filled to overflowing with them. Many came from their own Hogarth Press, for which they commissioned decorative dust-jackets from Vanessa Bell and many other artists. Sadly, the library was sold after Leonard's death in 1969, but the National Trust has filled the

shelves with copies of their works presented by the late Quentin Bell, the University of Sussex, and others.

Leonard made sure that there were flowering potted plants in the house – double begonias, gloxinias and lilies, brought in from the heated greenhouses, when they were at their best. The original hot houses fell into disrepair and were replaced by Leonard with the present greenhouse at the back of the house, so that the rooms would continue to be well stocked with plants.

Monk's House was always full of books. Vanessa designed the dust-jacket for *Jacob's Room* (1932) and most of her sister's other books

MONK'S HOUSE, RODMELL,
Equi-distant about 4 miles from Lewes and Newhaven.

CATALOGUE OF THE

Antique and Modern Furniture

Comprising: Mahogany Tall-boy Chest of 8 drawers with brass handles, Quaint Old Oak Chest of Drawers, Chippendale Washstands, Dressing Tables and Queen Anne Glasses, Old Carved Oak Chests, Corner Cupboards and Tables, Arm, Chippendale and other Old Chairs, Two Bureaux, old Copper Warming Pans, a Brass Dial Grandfather Clock, Wheel Barometers, Mahogany Office Table of 6 drawers, ditto cupboard.

AN INLAID SHERATON SIDEBOARD
Break Centre and Bronze Claw Feet.

Set of 5 Antique Carved Dining Chairs.
Old Inlaid Desks, Jewel and Work Boxes, A Sheraton Style Specimen Cabinet, Overmantels.

COTTAGE PIANOFORTE by Broadwood.
Old Decorative China and Glass. Clocks.

Electro Plated Goods. Bed and Table Linen.

Blankets, Down Quilts, Feather Beds and Bedding, Skin Carriage Rug, Brussels and Axminster Carpets, Linoleums, Hand Sewing Machine, Bagatelle, Croquet, Paintings, Engravings, Domestic and Laundry Items, Patent Mangle, Garden Tools and Implements, Wheelbarrow, Lawn Mower, an old Spring Cart and a quantity of miscellanea, which Messrs.

ST. JOHN SMITH & SON

(Having sold the property) have received instructions to Sell by Auction, upon the premises, on

THURSDAY, AUGUST 14th, 1919.
Commencing at 11 o'clock.
By Order of the Executors of Mr. Jacob Verrall, deceased.

On View the day preceding the Sale and Catalogues may be obtained of Messrs. ST. JOHN SMITH & SON, Land Agents and Valuers, 2, GLOUCESTER PLACE, SEAFORD (Tel. 187); 18, STATION STREET, LEWES and HIGH STREET, UCKFIELD (Tel. 18.

250/2/8/19.

The Woolfs bought three portraits of the Glazebrook family with the house: 'For myself, I don't ask anything more of pictures. They are family groups, and he began the heads very large, and hadn't got room for the hands and legs, so these dwindle off till they're about the size of sparrows claws, but the effect is superb – the character overwhelming' (letter to Margaret Llewelyn Davies, 17 August 1919)

Reclining nude; watercolour by Duncan Grant, 1919 (Bedroom)

7

The Sitting Room

In 1926 The Woolfs knocked down a central partition to create 'our large combined drawing eating room, with its 5 windows, its beams down the middle, & flowers & leaves nodding in all round us'. Here 'we sit, eat, play the gramophone, prop our feet up on the side of the fire and read endless books'. This remained the main room of the house until the upstairs sitting-room was added in 1929. After that date, it was used less frequently, but came into its own when the large family parties came over from Charleston.

The Woolfs furnished the room with an eclectic mixture of pieces dating from the 17th to the 20th centuries. The large painted table and the chairs, which bear Virginia's initials on their backs, were commissioned from Duncan and Vanessa in the early 1930s and recall their work for the Omega Workshops.

The canvas-work fire-screen was another commission, from Duncan, and was worked in cross-stitch by his mother, Mrs Bartle Grant, who was a skilled needlewoman. To the right of the fireplace is a bentwood chair designed by J.P. Hully and made by P.E. Gane Ltd of Bristol around 1937. The upholstered armchair beside it was one of Virginia's favourite reading chairs; it is covered in a modern reprint of a pattern designed by Vanessa for Alan Walton Textiles. The table in the centre of the room is topped with tiles painted by Duncan in 1930. The paintings include Trekkie Parsons's portrait of Leonard at Monk's House about 1950. Leonard bequeathed the house to Mrs Parsons, who had been a close friend since the early 1930s.

The canvas-work fire-screen was made by Duncan Grant's mother to his own design

The top of the large table was painted by Duncan and Vanessa in the early 1930s

Venus at her toilet: tiles painted by Duncan in 1930

The Sitting Room: Virginia had a particular fondness for green paint

The Dining Room

While their kitchen next door was being rebuilt in 1920, they were fed by the sexton's wife, Mrs Dedman, who lived nearby: 'The result is always savoury – stews & mashes & deep many coloured dishes swimming in gravy thick with carrots & onions'. Virginia was fond of game and light puddings, 'rich stews, the sauces. The adventurous strange dishes with dashes of wine in them'.

The Dining Room in its present form was created in 1929. The dining table was made in the early 20th century to a 17th-century pattern. The six dining chairs and the music cabinet to the left of the door to the Kitchen formed part of the furnishings of the Music Room designed by Duncan

and Vanessa that was exhibited at the Lefevre Gallery in 1932.

Mrs Grant made the canvas-work frame of the mirror to the left of the chimneypiece, again to her son's design, and gave it to Virginia as a Christmas present in 1937. Virginia thought it 'the loveliest looking glass I've ever seen'.

The Woolfs often played bowls on the large lawn behind the house, and the woods they used can be seen in a box under the stairs. Beyond them, to the right of the door, is the blue pottery bowl for the dogs' drinking water. On the music cabinet to the left is a dish made by Phyllis Keyes and decorated by Vanessa Bell. The porcelain on the chimneypiece is 18th- and 19th-century.

The canvas-work mirror frame is another example of Mrs Grant's work

(*Right*) Head of a Charwoman; by Vanessa Bell, c.1918–20 (Dining Room)

(*Far right*) Virginia Woolf in the sitting room of 52 Tavistock Square, the Woolfs' London home; watercolour by Vanessa Bell, 1935 (Dining Room)

(*Opposite*) The Dining Room

The Kitchen

The Woolfs rebuilt the Kitchen and installed a new range soon after they moved in, but the room was still prone to flood in wet weather. Virginia was proud of her bread-making skills, but resented any distraction from her writing. As she wrote in 1929, shortly after acquiring a new oil stove: 'At this moment it is cooking my dinner in the glass dishes perfectly I hope, without smell, waste or confusion; one turns handles, there is a thermometer. And so I see myself freer, more independent'. Leonard made the coffee and chopped up the dogs' food in here.

The cooking, however, was normally done by their servants. The Woolfs brought down Nelly Boxall and Lottie Hope from London as cook and housekeeper. Lottie stayed until 1924 and Nelly until 1934, when she was replaced by Louie Everest, who lived in the village and remained until Leonard's death. Trekkie Parsons's portrait of Louie Everest can be seen to the left of the dresser. She also painted the cupboard facing the garden door in the Charleston style. Leonard's initials appear below the standing figure.

Vanessa painted the two battered trays on the table under the window; they probably came from one of the London Artists' Association Christmas exhibitions in the late 1920s.

The Kitchen

Virginia Woolf's Bedroom

'A woman must have money and a room of her own if she is to write fiction'. Virginia was working on *A Room of One's Own* in 1929, while the extension, of which this room forms the ground floor, was being added by Philcox Bros. of Lewes. It was meant originally to be her work room, but 'I cannot yet write naturally in my new room, because the table is not the right height, & I must stoop to warm my hands. Everything must be absolutely what I am used to'. Instead, it became her bedroom, with a narrow bed by which she always kept pencil and paper in case inspiration should strike her in the middle of the night. She loved the austere brightness of the room and the sense of garden all around: 'I find that a sunny house is incredibly cheering.'

The tiles around the fireplace were decorated by Vanessa Bell and are inscribed 'VW from VB 1930'. The oval panel depicts a sailing ship with a lighthouse in the distance, recalling Virginia's novel, *To the Lighthouse* (1927). The late 19th-century silk embroidered Chinese shawl over the chair in the corner was given to her by Lady Ottoline Morrell.

Vanessa's painted tiles in the Bedroom feature a lighthouse, perhaps in honour of her sister's novel, *To the Lighthouse* (1927)

(*Left*) The Bedroom

13

The Garden

'The view across meadows to Caburn is before me now; & the hyacinths blooming, & the orchard walk. Then being alone there – breakfast in the sun – posts – no servants – how nice it all is'. Both Leonard and Virginia enjoyed gardening, but as Virginia explained, it was Leonard who became 'what I daresay is called garden proud', employing a full-time gardener with additional help and running four vegetable gardens, three heated greenhouses, beehives and an orchard. His choice of colour and plants was bold and bordered on the exotic.

In her short story, *'The Orchard'*, Virginia described a girl who dreams she is in heaven and wakes to find herself surrounded by apple trees in an orchard, and hears the voices of children. She was clearly inspired by the Monk's House garden and the sounds of the village school next door.

The garden falls into four contrasting sections. The formal walled area behind the house, the orchard to the south, the large open lawn to the east and the kitchen garden beyond.

The walled area is thought to have once been a piggery and its planting is disciplined by formal, straight-edged beds and paved areas decorated with sculpture. In the farthest section a fig-tree frames a cast of Stephen Tomlin's famous 1931 bust of Virginia (illustrated on p.1). On the same wall is Charlotte Hewer's 1968 bust of Leonard.

'Back from Monk's an hour ago, after the first week end – the most perfect, I was going to say, but how can I tell what week ends we mayn't spend there? The first pure joy of the garden I mean. Wind enough outside; within sunny & sheltered; & weeding all day to finish the beds in a queer sort of enthusiasm which made me say this is happiness' (diary, 31 May 1920)

Beyond is the orchard and, to the left, the Woolfs' bowls lawn. Beside the large round pond is C.H.N. Mommens's *Goliath* (c.1935). In the hedge separating the garden from the adjacent field once stood the two elm trees known as 'Leonard' and 'Virginia', under which their ashes were scattered. The first fell in a gale in 1943, and the second in 1985, the victim of Dutch elm disease.

The door to Virginia's bedroom

The cast of Donatello's *David* is now in the greenhouse; painted by Trekkie Parsons, about 1950 (Sitting Room)

Quentin and Angelica Bell playing bowls

The Lodge

The weather-boarded building by the churchyard was put up in 1934 to replace Virginia's previous writing room: 'There will be open doors in front; & a view right over to Caburn. I think I shall sleep there on summer nights'. Apples were stored in the loft above. After her death, the Lodge was doubled in size and used as a studio by Trekkie Parsons. The extension now houses an exhibition of photographs copied from the Monk's House albums, five volumes of snapshots of life at Rodmell taken by Leonard and Virginia. Through the glass screen can be seen the original writing room furnished with her desk and the blue writing paper she favoured.

The Lodge

Sitting outside the Lodge:
(from left to right)
Angelica, Vanessa and
Clive Bell, Virginia Woolf
and Maynard Keynes